Inventors

Designing and Creating Tomorrow's World

by Ruth Owen

Ruby Tuesday Books

Published in 2017 by Ruby Tuesday Books Ltd.

Editor: Mark J. Sachner
Designer: Emma Randall
Production: John Lingham

Photo Credits:
Alamy: 5 (bottom left), 5 (bottom right), 22; FLPA: 12; Getty Images: 7 (bottom), 9 (top), 17 (top), 24–25, 27 (top); Alex Goad (Reef Design Lab): Cover (center bottom), 20–21; The Ocean Cleanup: 10, 13 (center), 13 (bottom), 16, 17 (bottom); Public Domain: 9 (bottom), 11, 23, 26; Ruby Tuesday Books: 13 (top), 14, 27 (bottom); Shutterstock: Cover, 4, 5 (top), 6, 7 (top), 8, 10 (right), 18–19, 28–29, 30; Erwin Zwart (The Ocean Cleanup): 15.

Library of Congress Control Number: 2016907603

ISBN 978-1-910549-91-9

Printed and published in the United States of America

For further information including rights and permissions requests, please contact our Customer Service Department at 877-337-8577.

Contents

Inventing Our World

There's one thing that humans are very, very good at—inventing!

Almost everything around you was once someone's invention. Without an ancient inventor who discovered that crushed plant fibers could be mixed with water, squeezed flat, and dried, we wouldn't have paper. And without Johannes Gutenberg, who invented the printing press in the 1440s, paper couldn't be printed and turned into books, like the one you're holding. (By the way, if you're reading an ebook, then you have a whole other group of inventors to thank.)

From the first stone tools, invented by our early ancestors, to smartphones and robots, people have been dreaming, designing, making, and using inventions for millions of years.

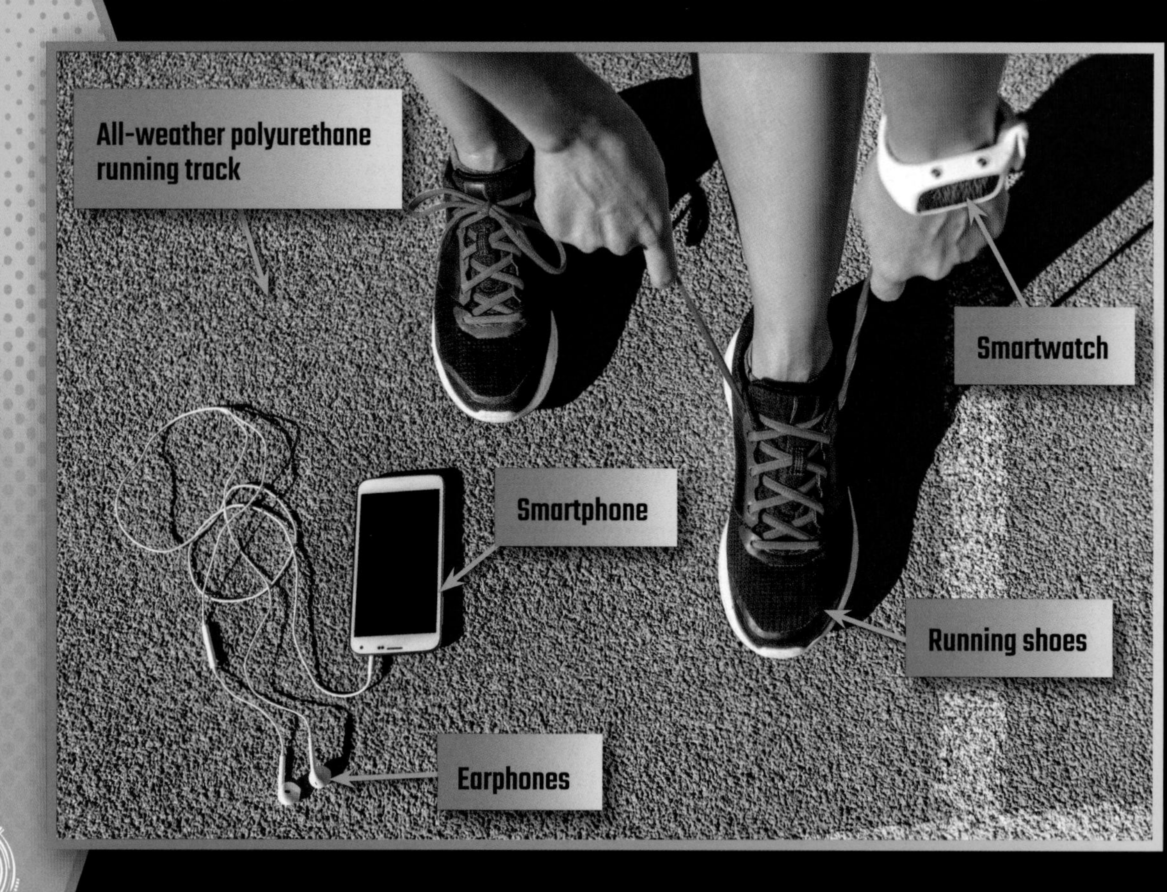

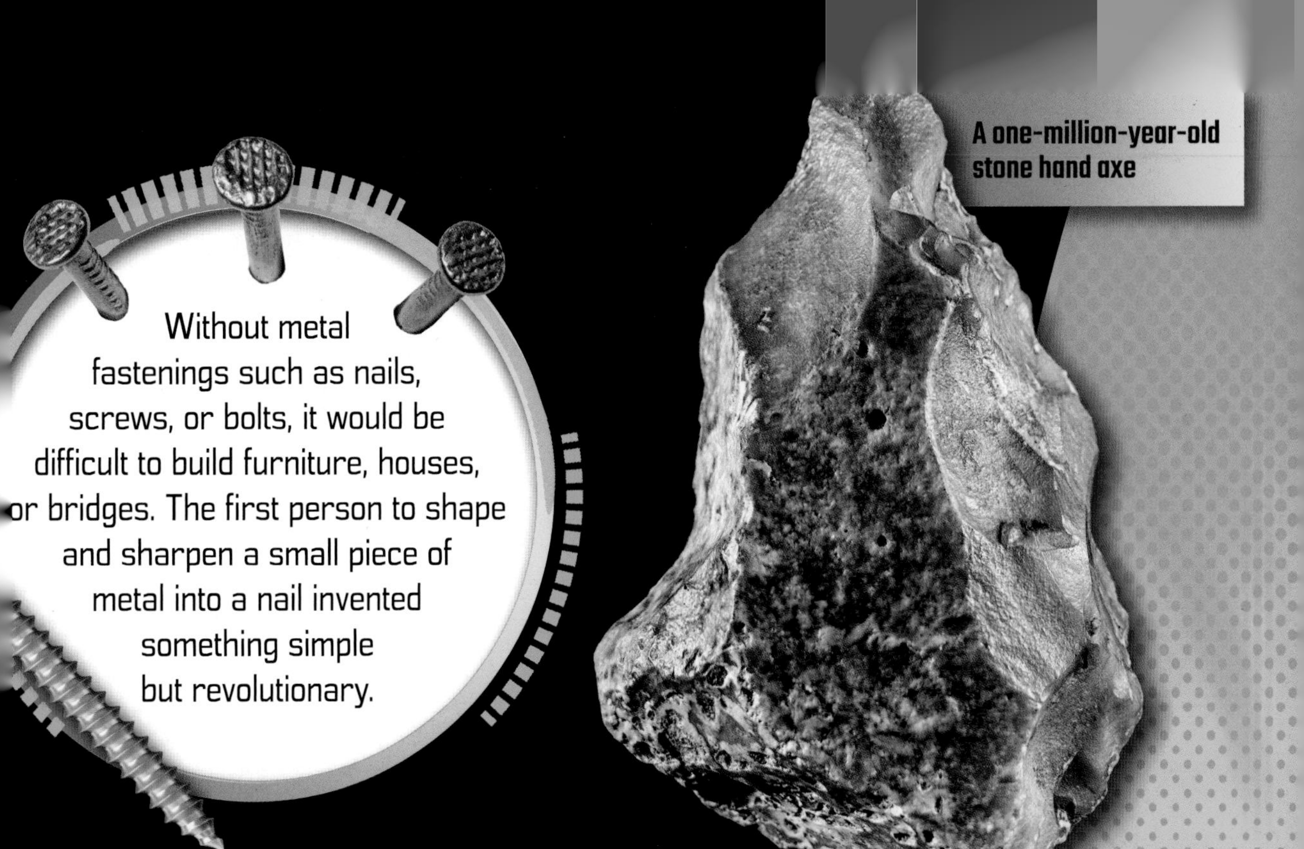

A one-million-year-old stone hand axe

Without metal fastenings such as nails, screws, or bolts, it would be difficult to build furniture, houses, or bridges. The first person to shape and sharpen a small piece of metal into a nail invented something simple but revolutionary.

In the late 1870s, Scottish inventor Alexander Graham Bell produced the first telephone that could transmit sounds.

A man using Bell's first telephone.

Today's inventors have designed smartphones that can be used for speaking, texting, going online, making movies, and even capturing virtual Pokémon creatures.

An Inventor's World

Is an inventor a scientist? An **engineer**? A **designer**? Usually, an inventor is all three of these things and more.

An inventor may be the first person to create an entirely new object or a new way of doing something. Sometimes, however, inventors create new and improved versions of things that already exist.

Inventors look at the world and see problems that need to be fixed. Then they work on invention ideas that could solve the problem. For example, shaking thick ketchup from the bottom of a glass bottle was always difficult. The solution to the problem was to invent an upside-down, squeezable plastic bottle.

An inventor using a 3D printer to produce a plastic object.

Inventors might do their work in **laboratories**, workshops, or offices. They may work alone, developing their own ideas, or be employed by a big company as part of a team in the R&D (research and development) department.

Inventors might use simple equipment such as a notebook and pencil. They also work with computers, electronics equipment, wood or metalworking tools, and 3D printers.

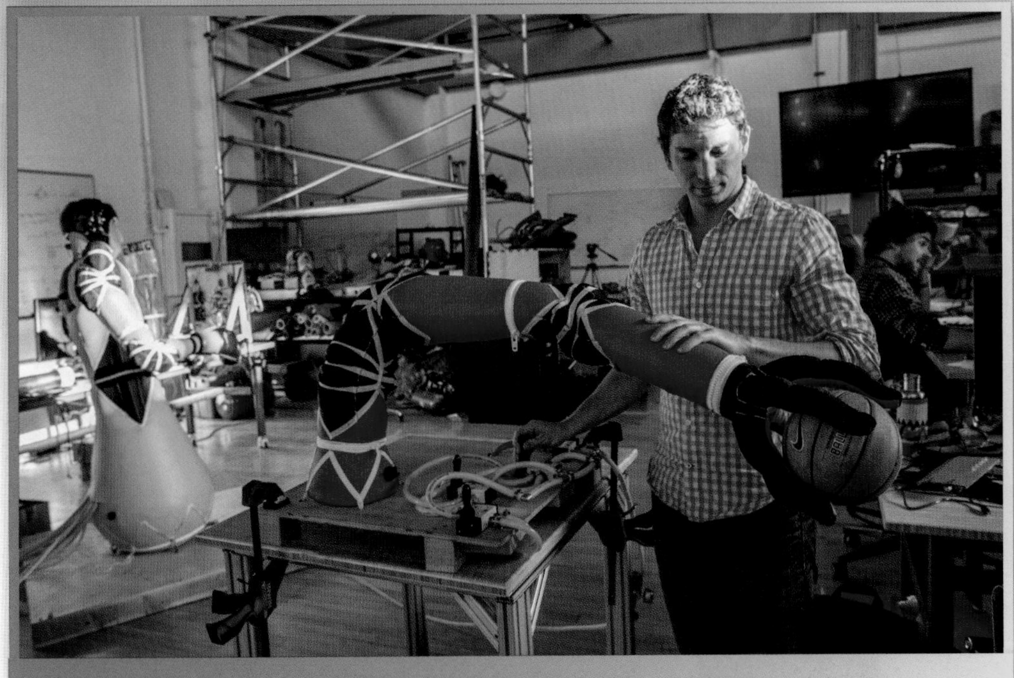

Engineer Kevin Albert works on a design for a robot with an inflatable body in his company's robotics laboratory.

An Invention Comes to Life

It's not enough to just have an exciting idea. An inventor must make the idea come to life.

Researching

Once an inventor has an idea, he or she must do research. Who will use the invention? What is the most **cost-effective** way to produce it? Are there older versions of the invention out there already? How will the inventor's new version be better?

Designing

Next the inventor gets to work on designs. He or she might sketch out designs on paper, or create them using a computer program. What materials will be used to make the invention? How will it work?

Every step along the way must be carefully recorded. Then, if something goes wrong, an inventor can retrace his or her steps to figure out what's not working.

Building and Testing a Prototype

Once the design is ready, an inventor builds a **prototype**, or test version, of the invention. The prototype may just be made from scraps of wood and metal. It doesn't have to look good. It just needs to show how the idea works. The prototype is tested and the results analyzed. The inventor should show the prototype to as many people as possible to get **feedback**.

Frank Nguyen (shown with his mother) wears the clunky prototype of his *HeartWatch* monitor that he built using a 3D printer.

When teenager Frank Nguyen's mother became ill with a heart condition, he invented a watch-like device that monitors a person's heart 24/7. If the device detects a problem, it calls 911.

Often the design doesn't work, but this is not a bad thing. When a design fails, it allows an inventor to redesign and improve the idea. Sometimes a mistake may lead to the accidental discovery of something exciting!

Ocean Cleanup: The Problem

Some inventors design a useful gadget or a fun toy. Others, like Dutch inventor Boyan Slat, take on larger projects. Boyan is tackling one of the biggest environmental problems our planet faces—ocean pollution!

Every year, about 8 million tons of plastic trash enters the oceans. Bottles and food packages discarded on beaches get washed out to sea. Rivers carry plastic bags and other garbage into the ocean. Shipping containers filled with plastic pellets, ready to be made into products in factories, are sometimes washed overboard from ships during storms.

Boyan Slat alongside trash recovered from the ocean. Boyan was still in high school when he began work on his plans to clean up the ocean.

These plastic pellets are the raw material that will be melted and shaped into plastic objects.

Ocean animals, such as fish, seabirds, and turtles, are killed when they eat plastic waste, thinking it's food. As bottles and other plastic items break down, harmful chemicals are released into the water.

When an animal eats plastic, its stomach cannot digest it. The animal's stomach becomes blocked, and it dies. Sometimes parent birds feed plastic to their young.

The remains of an albatross chick. The chick's stomach was filled with plastic trash, such as bottle tops and cigarette lighters.

Plastic trash does not decompose, or rot. It simply breaks down into smaller and smaller pieces. These tiny particles, known as microplastics, will remain floating in the ocean forever!

Ocean Cleanup: The Inventor

While scuba diving in Greece in 2011, Boyan Slat saw more plastic bags in the ocean than fish and other animals. He realized he wanted to do something to help solve the problem.

Many people work on prevention by campaigning and educating people to stop polluting the ocean. Boyan's solution was to find a way to actually clean up the ocean.

Ocean **currents** carry plastic waste into five main areas in the world oceans. The plastic accumulates in vast floating garbage patches, called **gyres**. Boyan got to work researching the issue as a scho science project. How much plastic is in the ocean? Does it only float at the surface or deeper down, too? Could a system be devised to capture the plastic waste within the gyres?

Turtles accidentally eat plastic bags because they think they are jellyfish!

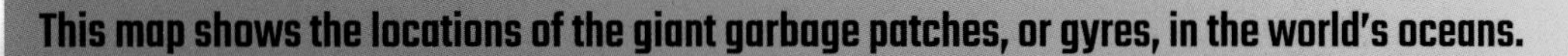

This map shows the locations of the giant garbage patches, or gyres, in the world's oceans.

No one knows exactly how large the North Pacific Gyre is, but some scientists believe it could be at least the size of Texas.

On research expeditions in Greece, Boyan trawled the surface of the ocean using a net system called a manta trawl. He could then analyze how much plastic was captured in the net and what size the pieces of plastic were.

Particles of plastic trapped in a manta trawl net

Ocean Cleanup: The Idea

Scientists have estimated it would take thousands of years to remove all the plastic from the world's oceans using boats and large nets. Boyan has come up with a system that will allow the ocean to help clean itself!

Boyan's invention is called the Ocean Cleanup Array. This V-shaped floating barrier will be positioned in a gyre. Then the ocean's currents will slowly funnel, or carry, the plastic waste into the V to an extraction platform.The plastic will be removed from the water and stored on the extraction platform. A boat will then visit the array about once every six weeks to collect the plastic from the platform and carry it back to land.

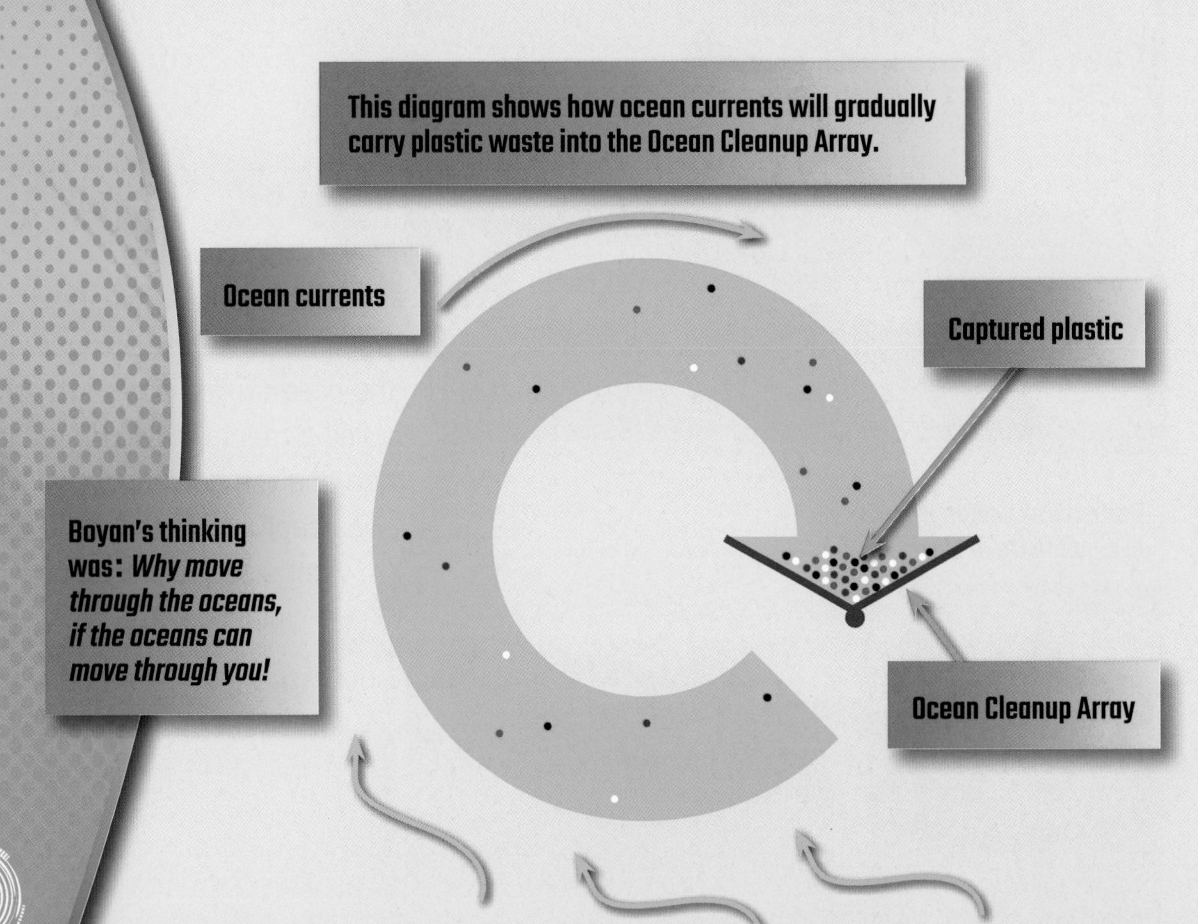

This diagram shows how ocean currents will gradually carry plastic waste into the Ocean Cleanup Array.

Boyan's thinking was: ***Why move through the oceans, if the oceans can move through you!***

This illustration shows how the Ocean Cleanup Array might look. The floating barrier will be 62 miles (100 km) long.

The plastic that's removed from the ocean will be sold to plastics recycling companies. Boyan calculated that the income from selling the recycled plastic will be more than the cost of setting up the project.

Ocean Cleanup: The Prototype

In 2013, Boyan started the Ocean Cleanup **foundation** to bring his invention to life.

Boyan and his team have tested small prototype arrays in tanks of water. In 2016, a 328-foot-long (100-m-long) prototype began testing in the North Sea off the coast of the Netherlands. The team wants to find answers to many questions, such as will the design work, and will it withstand bad storms? If something breaks or does not work, they will then make adjustments to the design and test it again.

Boyan's research showed that a single Ocean Cleanup Array could remove almost half the plastic trash in the North Pacific Gyre in just 10 years. He hopes to have the first array in action and cleaning up the ocean in 2020!

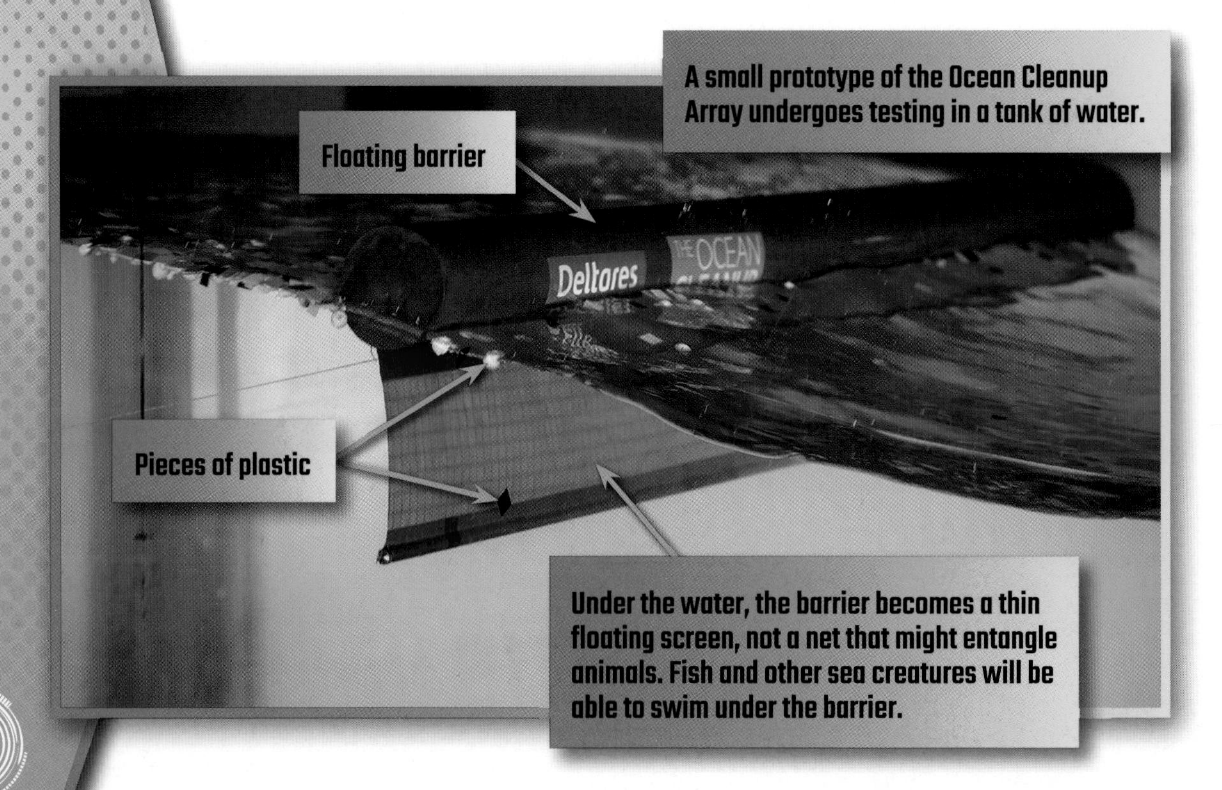

A small prototype of the Ocean Cleanup Array undergoes testing in a tank of water.

Under the water, the barrier becomes a thin floating screen, not a net that might entangle animals. Fish and other sea creatures will be able to swim under the barrier.

Boyan Slat with a section of the Ocean Cleanup Array prototype.

This section floats on the surface.

The underwater screen will capture floating plastic waste.

In 2014, Boyan Slat became the youngest-ever winner of the United Nations' Champions of the Earth Award for **inspiration** and action.

The North Sea Prototype is towed out to sea, ready to begin tests.

Disappearing Coral Reefs

Australian inventor Alex Goad began work on his invention as a university design project. Alex is an enthusiastic snorkeler and scuba diver, and he has invented a way to help rebuild damaged coral reefs.

Coral reefs are home to millions of species of ocean animals and other living things. These important natural habitats can take hundreds of years to form. Around the world, however, coral reefs are being destroyed, leaving the reef's inhabitants nowhere to shelter and find food.

Alex's idea was to design an easy-to-build, cost-effective way to create **artificial** reefs. Just as we replant trees to replace lost forests, Alex believes humans should help rebuild the reef environments that we've destroyed.

Coral reefs are home to plants and seaweed, and animals such as fish, turtles, lobsters, shrimp, sponges, and seahorses.

This rocky structure is made up of the skeletons of many generations of coral polyps.

Why Are Coral Reefs in Danger?

- Changes in ocean temperatures, due to climate change, can damage coral reefs.
- Vacation resorts build artificial beaches or boat marinas, damaging reefs near the shore.
- Fishing boats drag large nets (known as bottom trawling) along the seabed to catch fish. The nets rip up and damage reefs.
- Diving and sightseeing boats scrape or crush coral as they pass by overhead. Sometimes they drop their anchors into the coral, causing damage.
- Coral is collected to be sold as souvenirs to tourists.
- Pollution, such as oil, chemicals, and sewage, harms coral reefs when it is dumped in the ocean.

A coral colony is made up of thousands of tiny coral animals called polyps. A polyp has a hard outer skeleton that attaches to rock or the skeletons of other polyps. When polyps die, their skeletons remain, forming the rock-like structure of a coral reef.

Designing a Coral Reef

Building artificial reefs is not a new idea. Alex wanted to create a more natural design, however, and one that was easy to build.

Many existing artificial reef ideas were large structures that required big boats and heavy lifting gear to put them in place. Alex's system was inspired by Lego. It is called the Modular Artificial Reef Structure (MARS). A diver can position the small modules on the seabed and then slot them together—just like Lego pieces.

Alex's design means a new reef can be constructed in just a few days. During testing of the MARS system, small seaweeds, sponges, shrimp, and other living things made the modules their home within a few months.

When the MARS modules are slotted together they slow down water flow. This allows small animals to shelter inside the "reef," and particles of food to collect in the spaces.

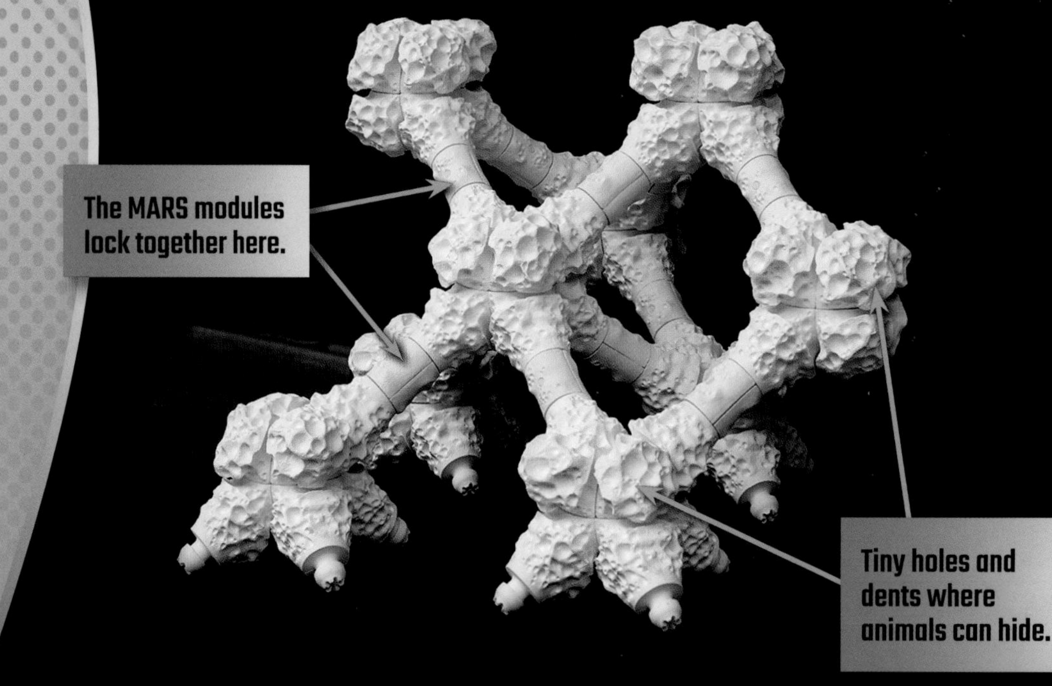

Alex hopes to sell the system to organizations that restore damaged reefs. The low-cost system could also be used by people living on small islands and in developing nations that have suffered damage to their natural coral reefs.

The modules are made of concrete covered with ceramic. During his research, Alex learned that living things are more likely to colonize a ceramic artificial reef. This is because ceramics and natural coral both contain calcium carbonate.

Keeping It Simple and Sustainable

British inventor Emily Cummins designs simple but clever objects that help improve people's lives. She works on inventions that are environmentally friendly and **sustainable**.

Every day, millions of people, mostly women and children, spend hours fetching water for their families. Often they must walk miles to reach a river, pond, or waterhole. Then they make the return journey loaded with heavy containers of water.

Emily designed a water carrier that can hold up to five containers and can be pulled along. Emily knew the people who most needed her invention might live in remote places with limited access to tools and materials. So the carrier can be made from branches and other pieces of wood that are free and easy to find.

These children are fetching water in Uganda, Africa. Emily Cummins' creative thinking will make this daily, back-breaking task much easier for many people.

Water Carrier Design

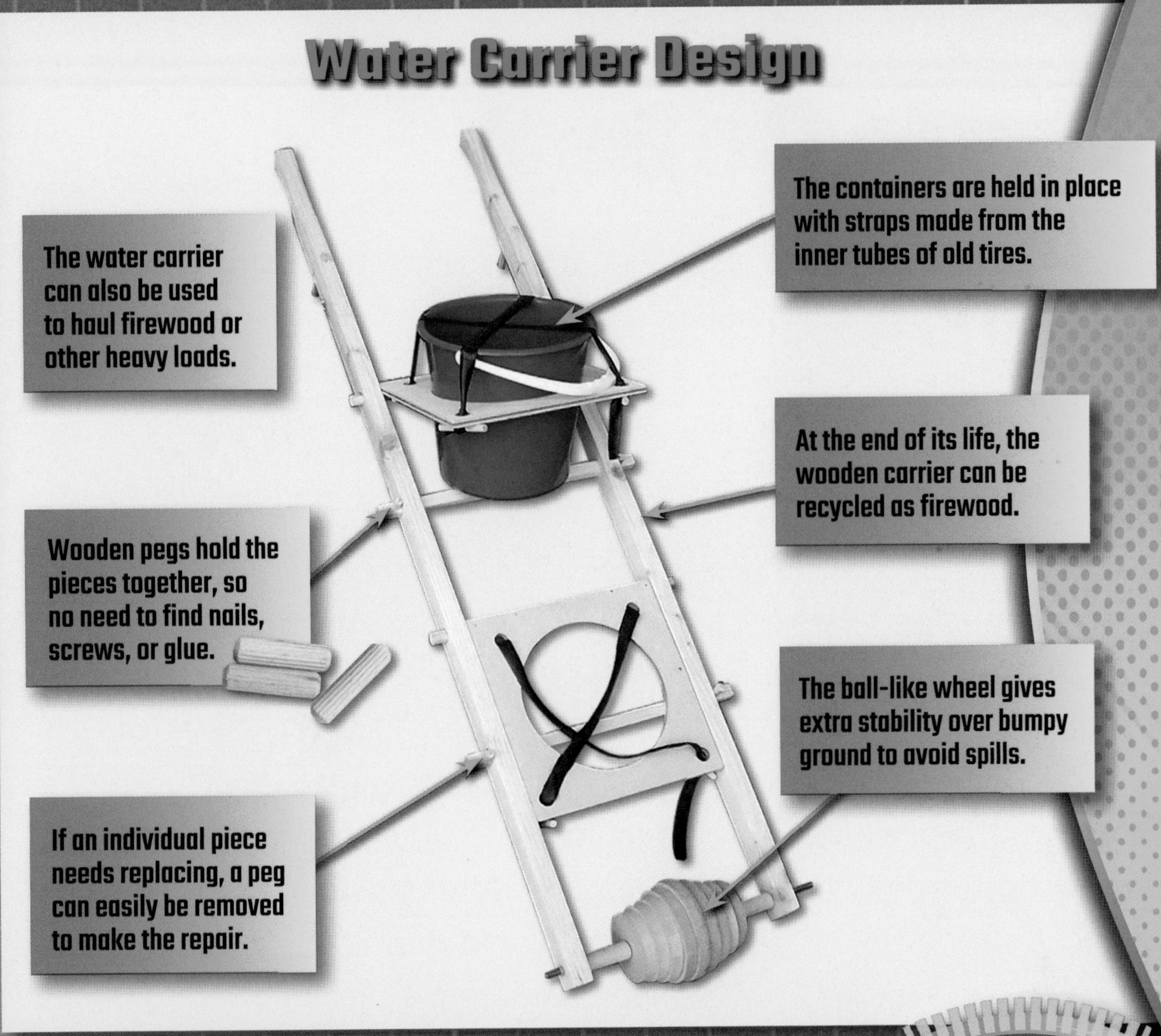

The water carrier can also be used to haul firewood or other heavy loads.

The containers are held in place with straps made from the inner tubes of old tires.

At the end of its life, the wooden carrier can be recycled as firewood.

Wooden pegs hold the pieces together, so no need to find nails, screws, or glue.

The ball-like wheel gives extra stability over bumpy ground to avoid spills.

If an individual piece needs replacing, a peg can easily be removed to make the repair.

Emily began her inventing career in her grandfather's toolshed when she was just four years old. She learned how to use tools to make toys out of scraps of materials she found in the shed.

Emily giving a talk about her work.

Escape the Earth

Some inventors take inspiration from science fiction to develop their futuristic ideas.

In 2006, a team of engineers and designers in the United States started a company called Terrafugia. The name is taken from the Latin words for "escape the Earth." Terrafugia's goal is to design, build, and sell flying cars!

The team is working on a four-seat vehicle called the TF-X. The TF-X won't need a runway. It will make vertical take-offs and landings in small spaces, such as parking lots and rooftops. It will fly at 200 miles per hour (322 km/h) and drive at highway speeds. Converting between drive and flight modes will take less than a minute. The Terrafugia team hopes the car will be ready for sale in the mid 2020s.

In the past decade, the Terrafugia team has successfully designed, built, and flown a prototype of a flying car called the Transition.

The Transition's wings fold up to the vehicle's sides.

The car will be a hybrid-electric car that runs on electricity and regular, unleaded gas.

Before flying in the TF-X, the driver will program the flight plan into the vehicle's onboard computer. Then, at the press of a button, the TF-X will automatically take off, fly to its destination, and land.

The TF-X will have two propellers that will allow it to take off and land like a helicopter.

Shooting for the Stars

For centuries inventors, scientists, and engineers have worked on telescopes and spacecraft that have allowed us to learn about space. Now we want to know if another planet like Earth exists beyond our **solar system**.

Alpha Centauri is the nearest star system to our solar system. In recent times, scientists have discovered planets in this system. However, at around 25 trillion miles (40 trillion km) from Earth, they are too far away for us to learn much about them. Even today's fastest spacecraft would take about 30,000 years to reach Alpha Centauri. So how do we get to investigate these distant worlds?

An ambitious project named Breakthrough Starshot hopes to one day send a fleet of ultra-fast **nano**-spacecraft to Alpha Centauri. Each of the tiny spacecraft will be no bigger than a credit card.

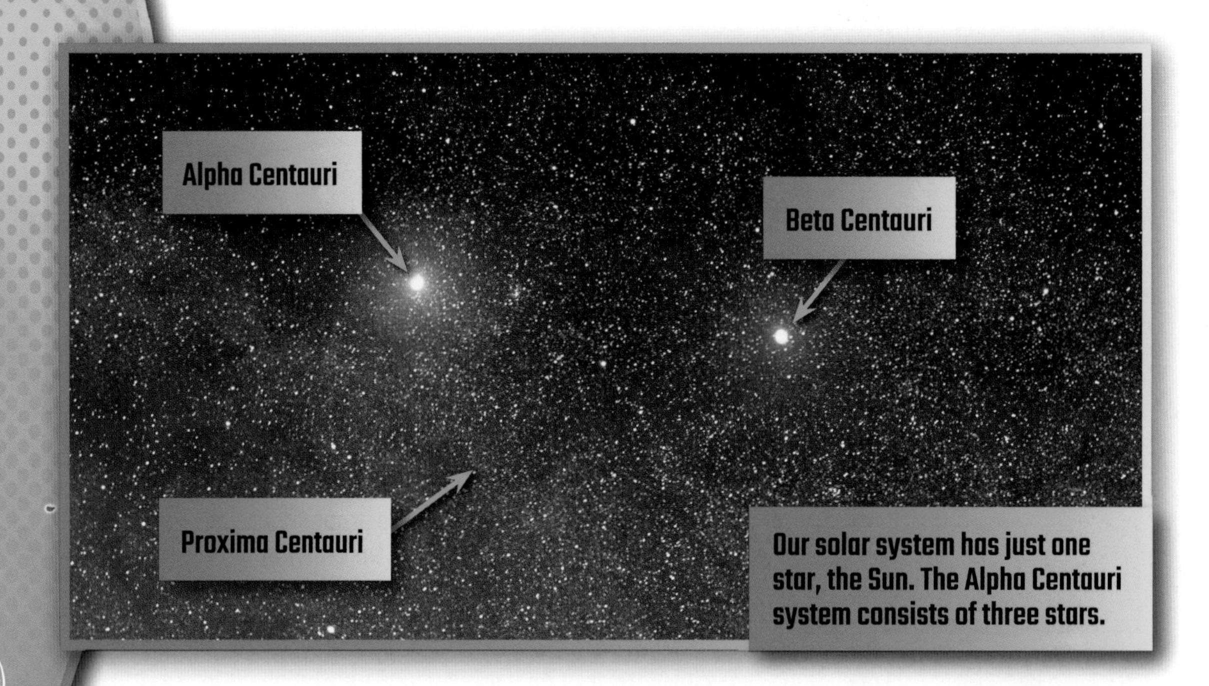

Our solar system has just one star, the Sun. The Alpha Centauri system consists of three stars.

The Breakthrough Starshot Project

The StarChip is an example of a nano-spacecraft.

The nano-spacecraft will be blasted into orbit around Earth inside a mother ship.

Once a spacecraft is released from the mother ship, light beamers on Earth will direct laser beams onto the craft's sail.

Each spacecraft will be attached to a thin piece of material called a lightsail.

Laser beam

Nano-spacecraft

The lasers will propel the tiny craft across space toward Alpha Centauri at ultra-fast speeds.

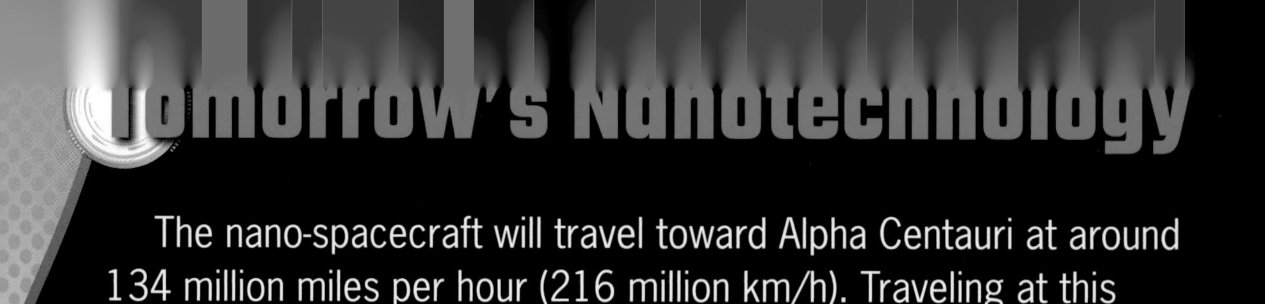

Tomorrow's Nanotechnology

The nano-spacecraft will travel toward Alpha Centauri at around 134 million miles per hour (216 million km/h). Traveling at this speed, they could reach Alpha Centauri in just 20 years.

The tiny spacecraft will be fitted with cameras and scientific equipment. They will collect information and take photos and then beam them back to Earth.

For now, Breakthrough Starshot is an exciting dream. If it does get off the ground, it will be thanks to the work of inventors, scientists, and engineers.

Inventors have given us the wheel, medicine, cars, planes, computers, and the Internet. Perhaps tomorrow's inventors will help give us our first glimpse of another Earth. Maybe even the first signs that we are not alone in the **universe**!

There are thousands of ways that inventors might be involved in a project like Breakthrough Starshot. They range from designing a tiny part of a spacecraft to inventing a new instrument that captures information about a distant planet.

Get to Work as an Inventor

Q&A

What qualities are needed to be an inventor?
An inventor should be:

- Determined to solve problems
- Curious
- Observant
- Creative and imaginative
- Good at paying attention to detail
- Persistent
- Willing to take criticism

What subjects should I study to be an inventor?
You can study math, art, and science, including computer science. In college, you might study chemistry, physics, biology, math, engineering, or computer science.

How soon can I get started?
Today! Inventing is a great hobby, and many inventors get started on their careers when they are still in school.

How do inventors earn money from their work?
Some inventors produce an object and then sell it through their website. An inventor might sell his or her idea to a large company. Then the company produces the object. Some inventors develop an idea that helps the planet or people in need. These inventors might set up a foundation, or charity, that raises money from businesses and the public so the invention can be put into action.

Protecting Your Big Idea

Once an inventor has developed an idea, the inventor can obtain a patent from his or her government's patent office. A patent is an official document. It says the inventor owns the idea and no one else is allowed to make or sell the invention without the inventor's permission.

What's Your Big Idea?

If an inventor can identify a problem that affects everyone, and it has not yet been solved, he or she could be onto a winning idea!

Try looking around you and identify an everyday problem in your home or school that needs to be solved. Can you invent a solution to the problem?

1. Begin your research by thinking about these questions.

   Who does the problem affect and how does it affect them?

   Are there any solutions currently available?

2. Think about ideas to develop. Once you've chosen an idea, begin work on a design, description, or plan. Remember that an invention can be an object or a way to do something. If your invention is an object, produce a sketch of the object and label all its parts. Make a list of the materials needed to make your invention.

3. Build a prototype, or model, of your invention. The prototype can be made from materials such as Lego pieces, modeling clay, cardboard, recycled plastic containers, or other scraps.

4. Write a short statement that explains how your invention will work and how it will solve the problem you identified.

Glossary

artificial (ar-ti-FISH-uhl)
Made by people; not natural.

cost-effective (kawst-uh-FEK-tiv)
Producing good results without it costing a lot of money.

current (KUR-uhnt)
A continuous movement of ocean water from one place to another.

designer (di-ZINE-ur)
A person who plans and creates the look of something, or how it will work.

engineer (en-juh-NIHR)
A person who uses math, science, and technology to design and build machines.

feedback (FEED-bak)
People's reactions to something. An inventor might show a product to people to get feedback on whether they like it or not.

foundation (foun-DAY-shuhn)
An organization (or charity) that raises money to do helpful work for people, animals, or the environment.

gyre (JIRE)
An area in the sea where ocean currents meet, causing a vast, slow-moving, rotating area of ocean.

inspiration (in-spuh-RAY-shuhn)
A source of ideas.

laboratory (LA-bruh-tor-ee)
A room or building where there is equipment that can be used to carry out experiments and other scientific studies.

nano (NAN-oh)
From the word "nanotechnology." Nanotechnology is science, engineering, and technological work that deals with very tiny, or microscopic, things.

prototype (PROH-tuh-tipe)
The first version, or test version, of something, such as a vehicle or machine. The final version is developed from the prototype.

solar system (SOH-ler SIS-tem)
The Sun and all the objects that orbit it, such as planets, their moons, asteroids, and comets.

sustainable (suh-STAYN-uh-buhl)
Something that will not stop but will continue in the future.

universe (YOO-nuh-vurss)
All of the matter and energy that exists, including all the planets, stars, galaxies, and contents of space.

Index

Read More

Colson, Mary. *Get Inventing! (Dream It, Do It)*. Mankato, MN: Heinemann-Raintree (2014).

Isabella, Jude and Matt J. Simmons. *Steve Jobs: Visionary Entrepreneur of the Digital Age (Crabtree Groundbreaker Biographies).* New York: Crabtree Publishing (2013).

Learn More Online

To learn more about inventors, go to:
www.rubytuesdaybooks.com/inventors